QUOTES
QUOTES TO INSPIRE & MOTIVATE

I0517469

By Paula R. Jumper

First Complete Quote Edition

"Such a simple yet profound work of art and creativity filled with jewels, Quotes to Inspire & Motivate, I can't put it down."

Marie Antionette Author of The Cook Chronicles,

Quotes

To Inspire & Motivate

Created by Paula F. Jumper

with Love

My intent is to motivate & inspire

also for you to remember me now and in the future

Dedicated to my miracle child

I love you always Shane Jumper

TABLE OF CONTENTS

Quotes To Inspire & Motivate

ISBN-13: 978-0-615-99862-6
ISBN-10: 0615998623
Library of Congress Cataloging-in Publication Data has been applied for.
Printed in the United States

Thank you so very much for just being who you are and allowing me to be who I am. The first step in getting to know me has now started. I want to get to know you as well. Open your mind and travel through this maze of mine inside a labyrinth of insightful creativity where knowledge is abounding. Our minds will connect, hopefully so will our hearts.

INTRODUCTION

Quotes to Inspire and Motivate are a reflection of my thoughts compiled into a small book to inspire and motivate. It is important for me to inspire through what I know and feel to be true based on my knowledge and experiences. Some of what I write is just me allowing you to get to know me and who I am, from wisdom, along with my writing journey that releases emotions, due to a thoughtful passion and inspiration. My aim is to inspire others the same. I want you to feel what I feel as well as think about people more. A good feeling does inspire, so why would I want to keep this enlightening experience to myself. Inspiration and motivation are so very much connected, when we are inspired it enacts us to be motivated. Motivation to me is exact transcending from inspiration; it is indeed the final outcome for action. Let us begin with the conscious thought that will, hopefully, plant the seed and move us to work. I love to feel a friendly love and what is real. I want us to love each other. We are more alike than we think. All I have done is put these inspiring and motivational thoughts as well as help you to get to know me personally on paper. So we can refer back to them when we need inspiration in our lives, regardless if this endeavor has come about through my aspirations. I would like to add that this is only the first edition, and my hope is that our journey is continued.   Thank You!

Quotes

To Inspire & Motivate

By Paula R. Jumper

QUOTES By Paula R. Jumper

Motivational

The motivator is more than a word,

it is the doer without having to do anything

except inspire.

Motivation moves us to action

just by what can be observed or spoken.

Deriving from the word motive

the word still does not need

a reason or validation.

It is what it is and does what it does.

I am a motivator,

become a motivator along side of me !

TO INSPIRE AND MOTIVATE

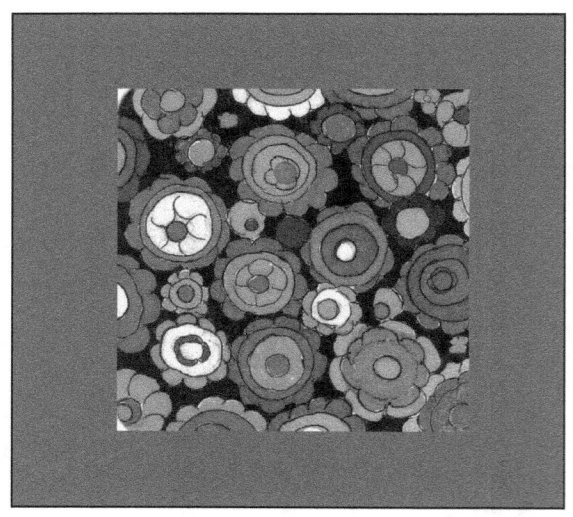

QUOTES By Paula R. Jumper

A masterpiece may take a little time to complete. It doesn't mean it's not worth completing, especially if it's with someone you love or something that you love doing.

The sweet taste of that 1st dollar made from creativity and hard work is as green as fresh produce to my digestive system.

It is more than a feeling that will give satisfaction to prosper. It is the action that you take to make the feeling prosperous.

I'll never stop explaining, I guess it's the teacher in me that feels no details should be left out.

3

<u>When your state of mind and spirit is right everything else will follow.</u>

A man or woman that reads is a ready man or woman. A man or woman that writes is exact. I didn't put quotes because it is in my head, but maybe not word for word. By Marcus Garvey

<u>When sleeping women wake mountains move, I don't know who wrote it. but I've been there and I was this woman.</u>

<u>So that you don't become what you believe, believe what you want to become.</u>

The way I feel is like bad things are a triple effect, but good things are too.

If the rain could talk, I believe it would wash away the troubles of yesterday. Your tears would be no more. Embrace the rain for it is powerful but good as well.

True persistence and determination can turn a seemingly defeat into a victory. May your heart's desire and passion meet its purpose and be fulfilled, Love Paula

Keep hope alive. When it seems all hope is gone. Hope is the slightest light in a flame that never dies. Never give up on hope and it won't give up on you.

It's better to start small than to not start at all. A small effort can eventually make a big difference.

The hardest part is getting started.   The best part is finishing what you start

Very few prefer not call the term alone lonely, yet a form of solitude they welcome as meditative prayer, and wouldn't have it any other way.

A warm hug, a simple kiss, a sincere smile, or a soft gaze. All these components ignite chemistry that equal friendliness from me to you, on a good day of course.

A good person can make you feel good when you aren't. Good people know you're smarter and better than you think you are. They know!

I like the way a chain of events create a domino effect or how the cards lay. You never know what will turn up.

A few words can mean as much as many, silence can have no meaning and be plenty.

Things are never the way they seem to be. God knows the true heart.

Live, Love, and Cry, it's good to cleans the soul.

If water is life, then the wind must be the air we breathe. If the trees are history then the ground must be foundation. Let us keep our feet on solid ground then our circle of life is worthy of our earth's oxygen.

May knowledge you acquire touch your soul to be compassionate and not just knowledgeable.

It doesn't always matter what people think of you. What matters most is what you think of yourself.

God has the power, strength, wisdom, most of all love to make it better. Faith moves mountains

Sometimes things are just not as bad as they seem. You may think you're a villain, when actually you may have just made a mistake.

Out of nothing can come something miraculously. Believe it can happen miraculously. I know this to be true I have seen it.

Label yourself your way, you don't have to accept a label you didn't ask for or want.

When you can't shake that feeling and nothing helps, not even talking or talking to yourself, prayer will help you before and after you hit rock bottom. I know this, pass it on

Know yourself, and know what you know about yourself. If you don't know yourself, you don't know who you are, by Socrates in my own words.

May your equilibrium stay balanced, and the weight of life stay equal so that it may not hold you down. Obstacles may arise through push and pull, stay steady to become stronger

Take that walk in the rain like someone put a sign on your back, Let the rain splash me. The umbrella won't always protect you or keep you dry.   One side may get wet, but its ok, just kept walking. If you feel like a duck be a happy duck. If you feel cool than be that too. Do what you want to do, as long as you feel good about you. Hold your head up and have courage, It will get better.

Sometimes it's not always what you say, but what you don't have to say that's important.

Sometimes something bad can happen, and something good can follow. Strange but true.

Today was a good day, the rain sounded good this morning. Tell yourself how thankful you are. It's so easy to take things for granted big or small.

Never assume you know a person because what you think you know or may not know might surprise you.

11

Whatever is working in your life, keep doing what you're doing if you can. The reason is your doing something right.

It's just as hard to do nothing as it is to do something when your use to being busy. Remember thinking still counts for something.

Fill your life with color and saturate it with love and bring more contrast. Feel the temperature, while rising with brightness in the art that is you full of value. Color your first picture, make it an illuminating day. Let me see the color in your life transcending the dark side in me. I still love black it will always accent my life.

It's the secret person of the heart that is more attractive than a person's outside appearance.

God gave us freedom to not be an anarchy people and be controlled like robots.

It only takes that one special thing in your life to make everything seem right, so for all the things that have gone wrong keep holding out for that one special feeling.

Make your good outweigh your bad, this way it is easier for you and others to forgive you.

Sometimes the fruit doesn't fall to far from the tree of bad apples, it doesn't mean you have to become that bad apple if you work hard not to. You are not your parents.

When I look up in the sky I am in awe by what I see. It's not just the birds or the clouds and the vastness. It's kinda scary yet amazing

Thinking is more than just a thought, it is yours to keep or share. I appreciate it.

Change is not always easy. Change in a good way can never hurt to try.

14

There is beauty in a blank page. If you like mystery than you will love making the page come alive.

Trust is a funny thing when you've been hurt. It's not always easy to realize a person wants to support you in a good way.

Be understanding, don't give up on an untrusting person.

We are all striving for something.   As long as it's positive and good, strive to be who you say you are and want to be.

TO INSPIRE AND MOTIVATE

Inspirational

Nothing in life is as enjoyable as inspiration.

Catch it and become infected by it. Inspiration is
indeed all around.

Become an inspiration to all you come in

contact with.

Inspire to become inspired

TO INSPIRE AND MOTIVATE

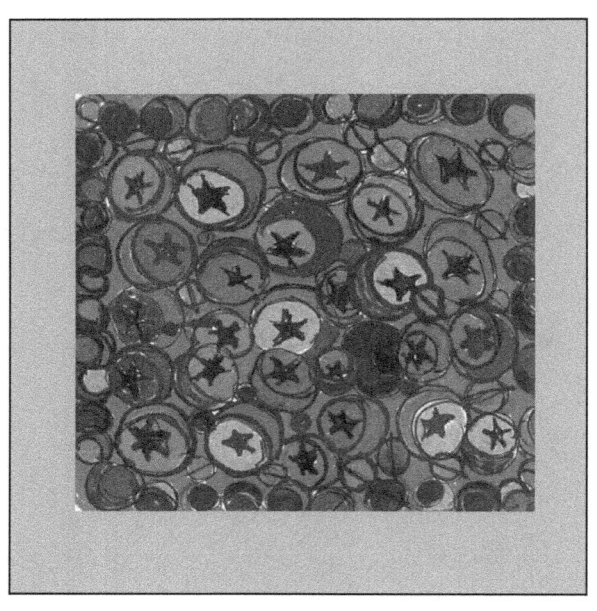

A professor that cares about young people who are underprivileged. My kind of man, a teacher and a man with a heart of gold.

I wasn't always beautiful. I was a diamond in the rough. My beauty is from the inside out. When I am both only then am I complete.

Good conversation needs great communication at least I do, I thrive with it.

Work hard as if you're working for God and you deserve to eat. Hard work will get you far.

When you're smiling it's good. When you make someone else smile its better.

The longer it took me to become a woman, the more seasoned and complete I became. The aroma of essence is sweetest when it's with its own elements.

I can see a stone in all its simplicity. Simplicity is the origin of all things sensational to me.

What may have not meant something to me, may have meant the world to someone else. I am very careful how I treat people because not everybody thinks the same or functions the same.

When I really like what I'm doing, I put effort in it, and I work on it till I get it right. That's me 100%. When you do whatever you like that's when you will put the most effort into it.

QUOTES By Paula R. Jumper

If you wanna know who I have become look at my past. If you wanna know who I am, then look at me now. You can't figure me out unless you look closely because I'm more than what you see.

She works from sunup to sundown, even after hours. She is a good woman but tired.

I love an Afro any day. No afro is a bad afro. Short or big as long as it's an Afro I'm wearing it proud

I'd rather wait on time than rush to change time. This way I know my time is mine.

21

<u>Imagination is the key to creativity and
originality. My imagination constantly
changes. You will never really know me like I
know myself.</u>

<u>I dream I'm running and flying when I'm
swimming in emotions</u>

<u>Everybody needs someone to talk to at some
point, make yourself available to someone who
needs you at the right time.</u>

<u>To all the woman who raised me I thank you
because it took a village. Thank you to the village
who raised my son.</u> I love you for your
contribution to me especially you Terry and my
Aunt Cheryl. Thank you mom for birth and now
friendship.

22

<u>Next time you go to the store be happy to be
buying food. Dance to the music just because.</u>

If my imagination soars on a train Imagine what
a plane could do.

My focus is my weakness and my strength.
I am deep yet I am also real. God and life have
humbled me, but my friends have taken a back
seat and I apologize.

You know you have done a good job with your
kids when they start to sound smarter than
you are. Now just let me see my youngest son
who is seventeen become a man, before I am
gone and not after.

23

TO INSPIRE AND MOTIVATE

On Time PJ Ready Portraits, aka butter fox, Poetess, PJ love, design Artist. I'm Just Authoress me and my imagination, Smooth like butta, and crazy like a fox, I am a rose inside a deep red heart that bleeds a purple kiss. write this on my obituary

I love my hair it is the representation of me. I am woman, a warrioress woman. A warrior like Samson that held the power in his hair. Now you know, and you know it was impossible without God. Let me hook you with my locks

What is soft as a baby and has the power to soothe you? it is my lips soft words and my kiss that speaks. Let me gracefully dance my way into your heart.

QUOTES By Paula R. Jumper

When people can't see my worth, I will always
know that I am worth way more than they can
see.

My hair is the epitome of me. I was rooted in my
nappy roots, because they ridiculed me and
couldn't see my beauty, now I shine just the same.
Ladies you know who you are. I'll never forget
you. However I forgive you and thank you.

I never question my faith in God only my
actions.

African dance and spirituality are one in the same
a great experience

There will be people who won't believe you've changed. No explanation is needed, you're alright with me and I believe you. I have seen you from the beginning . I know it's true that change is real.

Waiting all day for the wake of my pens energy to call me to come dream. I am moved by the love of my art just like sex, I'm doing it again and again, Watch out because here I come.

My dog is our friend, we love him his name is Bart., he is also our watch dog and protector

Particles of my life have materialized into poetry.

I love my afro, like I love being black!

Drenched and exhausted, curled up in a ball with my head lying on the side of the table, is how I will be when you find me. I work hard even when I am tired.

Yes, you can draw me PJ, Sketch me the same as I look. No sketch me beautiful. Make me different, make me unique are sounds I like to hear.

You see the head scarf I wear, then you see my serenity. This is who I am, so accept me without reason. I feel like the queen that I am. I've been this way along time, and I don't plan to change my adornment any time soon.

I am a teacher and I bet you didn't know it. We all need teachers in our lives, just please let the teachers be good teachers. Teaching by example is the best kind of teaching, when it comes right down to it.

<u>Finding a good teacher is like finding a treasure.</u>

<u>Don't be afraid to speak if you can, it might be your last chance. I was a poet and neither did I know it. If you know it show it, if it's in you it will come out.</u>

<u>A few words can make a big difference in a lifetime, because a few people cared I write a few words.</u>

28

<u>I never wonder if what I like is good I know if I like
it someone else does too.</u>

She was a young girl playing the part of a
woman. Her maturity showed where ever she went.
Everyone loved her, she wasn't promiscuous, only
mature because she had to be. People trusted her
with their kids, although she was not a woman.
She was the big sister your children loved and she
loved them too.

TO INSPIRE AND MOTIVATE

QUOTES By Paula R. Jumper

Words of Wisdom

Nothing is more priceless than Wisdom not even
gold or love.

Love can capture a person's heart.

Gold can bring fortune.

Wisdom can encourage a people to love.

TO INSPIRE AND MOTIVATE

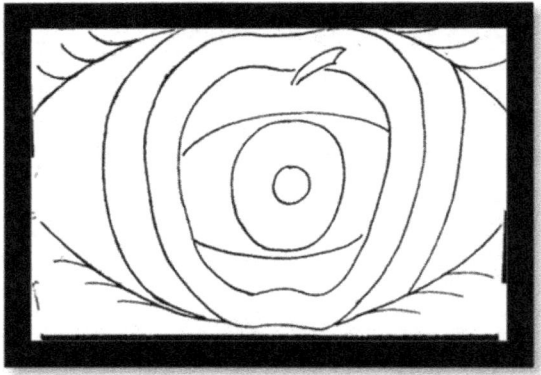

Rejection is never easy, but knowing rejection will never defeat you, if you know who you are is.

It's not always that person who you see as the favorite, that is the most worthy, on the other hand they could be. The point is not always.

The soul of a man never changes. The soul of a man is the man.

What we take for granted someone else wishes they had. If we had everything we would appreciate nothing.

Everything positive isn't without negative, two energies can exist together, sometimes creating an effect that connects the two effectively..

I find a strong similarity in the sweet taste of success and no pain no gain. If you can get from one to another it feels good.

We may know something, it doesn't mean we don't need reinforcement, regardless how simple or old it may be.

God gives us the tools, it's up to us to want to use them A person may show you the side they want you to see, doesn't mean that's who they are all of the time.

QUOTES By Paula R. Jumper

<u>You don't really know a person unless you take the time to get to know them or have the time</u>

<u>A person can use big words or have a fancy title, it doesn't mean they are a good person or smart about things in life that matter.</u>

"Just because a woman is sleeping don't mean she is sleep." I stole this off the back of some man's shirt that said the word man instead of woman. The difference is he wore it on the back of his shirt and I would have worn it on the front.

35

You don't really know a person unless you take the time to get to know them or have the time. I know at times I can be guilty.

Change is inevitable nothing can stop the will to change. Prepared or not it's coming.

Children see things bigger than we do, be careful of the impact you expose on them.

Beautiful gardens are planted by minds that sprout into flowers of accomplishment.

People and things are temporary but Gods love is forever.

I realize that when you run out of things to say you start telling your personal business.

It's not always what you say but what you don't have to say that counts.

Nothing like a beautiful Sunday morning, even when it's snow on the ground.

Change is not always easy. Change in a good way can never hurt to try.

I am so glad not all things are etched in stone. Having the ability to change your mind at the right time is not a crime.

<u>Sometimes the rain makes one dance inside out. Treasure these moments.</u>

Words to live by, "control your body and don't let your body control you". "The most important thing about work is being there". Two important quotes in my life that didn't take much thought but mean a hell of a lot to me.

<u>It is important to hold your tongue, all though sometimes it isn't always easy.</u>

Someone you know or love may have a disability but they may also have a gift.

Once in a while good advice can come from a not so smart person's mouth, anyone can give a witness and make a difference.

Nobody is as good as you think they are, and that's alright because neither are you.

A person who knows both, the comfortable life and the poor, better relates to people. Experiencing both situations surely makes them know the difference first hand.

The best way to rid yourself of a problem is to get rid of it completely.

Silence can have no meaning and be just as pleasing.

Do you really think you know who you really are? Or are you surprised at what you see when you are challenged and find out you don't.

What the naked eye doesn't see is obvious through the third eye. You can't see a prize inside a box until it is revealed

I am a firm believer in honesty, but do people really have to be so honest as to hurt a person's feelings, I don't think so. Do please remember to apply the golden rule.

When the dust has settled. When everything's calm. When you think she has forgotten. Think again. Never underestimate a woman.

When it rains it pours. A troubled rain can bring a flood of struggles.

An ambitious person can see a goal. A person with determination will make it happen.

Fear is not all bad, to have none is worse. Sometimes our inflictions save us from ourselves.

It may take only an hour if you know and believe something to make a decision , or a lifetime if you're not sure.

Accepting what we see and here without safe guarding our minds and hearts is when we fall prey to accept any and everything.

History is like a shadow that follow you, repeating if you let it.

<u>Fairytales and dreams have strong
distinction together. One evolves into another
through stories.</u>

<u>Children need a lot of love and discipline too.
love will cover it all. Love is the answer</u>

Sometimes you just gotta let it do what it do
and say what you wanna say. The difference
is they thought about it but you said it.

<u>Little girls grow up , be careful what you do,
especially when they are the epitome of you.
Scary but true.</u>

It is ok to be modern with new technology, it is not ok to rob one of originality, creativity and imagination that can never be replaced.

I don't believe you can teach consistency it has to be practiced and then learned.

Never assume you know a person because what you think you know or may not know might Surprise you.

Sometimes people want to make you look bad to make themselves look good. That's right I said it.

<u>It doesn't always have to be the parents fault</u>
<u>because a child may not be as good as the</u>
<u>parent. How can you guide them if they won't</u>
<u>let you?</u>

<u>Courage may be our strength and aggression</u>
<u>can be our weakness, although we still need</u>
<u>both in this world to survive.</u>

<u>We may know something, it doesn't mean we</u>
<u>don't need reinforcement, regardless of how</u>
<u>simple or old it may be.</u>

We wear the mask that grins and lies, with
torn and bleeding hearts we smile. But let the
world dream otherwise. These are excerpts I
took from poetry by Paul Lawrence Dunbar. If

you can't actually see it, feel it or breathe it, including what I write, it's still a mask. We wear the mask! Face book cell phones, text messages too.

Everyone came into our lives for a reason, but they do not determine the outcome of our fate. Thank you God for that.

They say don't go shopping when you're hungry, I say don't make a decision when you're tired or have been drinking, although I still write through the night and long for that drink. I just don't waste my time and money going shopping when I'm hungry.

To be a master you need to first be a servant.
You can't be the boss without earning your
status.

There is nothing more attractive than
acuteness, intelligence and wisdom they never
fade.

One step backwards means two steps forward
reversed. When I come back I wanna come
back stronger.

It's better to start small than to not start at
all.

<u>A small effort can eventually make a big difference.</u>

Parents make a big impression on their children. It's a blessing to have a good parent.

If we love our bodies like we say we do, then we will feed it what it needs instead of what it doesn't, it's not easy believe me, neither is trying to control the flesh instead of it controlling you.

One of the most important thing about work is being there.

It's ok to have a best friend as long as you're not the only friend who knows it.

Words to live by, control your body and don't let your body control you.

It is better to have a duck that looks, acts and quacks like one than a fake one. You can even be an ugly duck just be real.

Imagination is the key to originality.
You don't really know who you are unless you know yourself

TO INSPIRE AND MOTIVATE

QUOTES By Paula R. Jumper

Love

Feel it , Breath it, Need it

We all have to nave it.

Without Love we cannot exist.

Love can be bad or good.

True Love is everything

worth being loved and more.

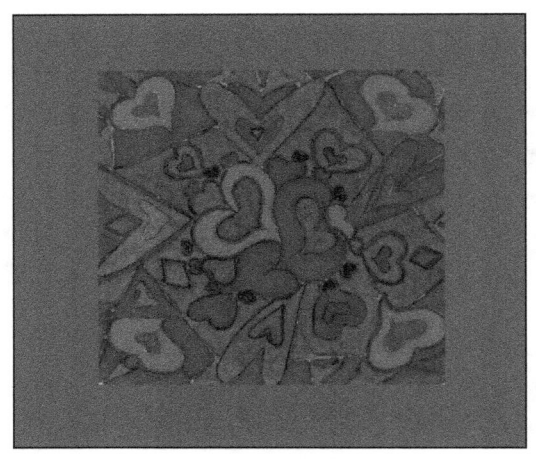

True love takes time to grow and know a person. It's not like a one night stand that hit ends before it begins.

Sometimes I get tired, although I never get tired of the ones who truly love me in my life. Some people stay on my mind like a beautiful sunset, and others remain in my heart where love comes and goes like the rain. I only love what is beautiful and true. I am the rain that loves the sun, its one in the same.

It is not the explanation of a feeling or the definition of love that determine what love is. Love has to be shown in order to be truth.

In a relationship, I can tell a woman's worth by the time he spends on his woman, his woman's worth is worth his time. Goes both ways. A woman's worth is ideal. Define me be by my idea.

I believe in the connected. We all need a connection in our lives that makes us feel valued. We are all connected in some way, form or fashion. Believe in the connected with love. Now you have a connection to hold on to.

People and things in this world are temporary, but God's love is forever, present life and the next.

"A thin line between love and hate." If we can make war we can make love". Two of my favorite quotes

Appreciation is just love on a small scale. I appreciate the love. I appreciate you. Love PJ

My love is transparent strong like a bull, and as soft as a dove. Come to me will protect you like a lamb in the bosom of a Lion. let me spread my wings around you, my eagle within will protect you.

Rain fall down on me, I got a thing for the rain. Make it rain all day, My tears of pain will burst into you like a river you will never escape me or my love, hold on I got you!

My love is like a sunset even when it's gone it's still there.

He calls me kiss, he enchants me with his words, I need more than the sweet sentiments of this, I need action to exemplify his words.

When love is in the air it's intoxicating. I love to spread my love energies for you to breath.

Is it not good enough to love God or do we need to love God with our whole heart mind and soul?

It is better to learn how to love before you learn to have sex. Having sex and making love means more when you really love a person.

We can help each other stay spiritually grounded as well as emotionally. I need it and I want to be there when you need it.

like glue I'ma stick to you, we fit like a glove hand in hand baby.

If you can't be with the one you love than love yourself, God loves you and I have love for you too.

Love plus action are omnipotent.

Give me flowers it tantalizes my senses. Give them to me often to captivate me.

57

<u>People and things are temporary, but Gods love is forever.</u>

I'm hooked like passion in my lips. He is a rough black diamond and blue pearl. His every word hangs over me. Our friendship has no ultimatum. Time has no measurement with us.

Keep watching me and you will see, I love you is all you really needed to know. The answer to your questions will be revealed in the end.

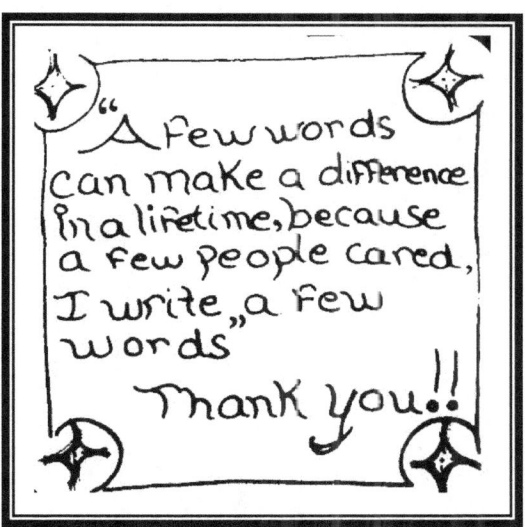

"A few words can make a difference in a lifetime, because a few people cared, I write „a few words"

Thank you!!

TO INSPIRE AND MOTIVATE

QUOTES By Paula R. Jumper

Just Me

I can only be me,

no one else, Who would I be anyway,

I am comfortable with myself.

TO INSPIRE AND MOTIVATE

I go when I wanna go. I eat when I wanna eat;
I sleep when I wanna sleep, and I think how I
wanna think . I'm a grown ass woman
making my own grown woman decisions.

I don't like people who pretend to be your friend
then pretend they never knew you. I don't like
fake people.

I don't like when a person uses another person
as an excuse for their own mistakes, especially
those who claim so much obedience. Don't test
me unless you're God.

I prefer music to sooth my soul even in the
elevator or on the phone. There is also a
savage beast in me that needs music as well.

He reminded me of my leather black jacket and black purse where I keep my poems. I am his black cat in the night only he can tame me and make me purr by Paula

<u>I use to always try and find the good in people until I realized everybody just aren't good people.</u>

If I got a problem and you got a problem that I don't have, maybe we can come together and help solve it. Just make sure I don't have the same problem you got.

Riding my bike and looking sexy, I am in my element and loving it,

If it's not complicated it's simple. I don't want to be simple minded.

I like to laugh when I'm feeling sad it turns my frown upside down.

I can't always see weeds until they start to grow. I guess its just nature's way of telling me something doesn't belong.

My body lets me know when it's tired. I am so glad my mind feels the need to keep being exercised.

A turkey burger with chopped fresh spinach, mushrooms, and onions. A sister gotta eat, and you know it, that I like good food.

<u>I'd like to be childlike to think as a child, and still be free to be me and dream as an adult.</u>

Sometimes I make a fool of myself or talk when I shouldn't, but I always know what I'm going to say when I say it. I say it anyway because the thing that matters the most is what I think of myself.

Watching a person who is so much talented then you are makes you want to be better, after you feel like crap of course.

QUOTES By Paula R. Jumper

<u>My days are shorter not longer, I'm happy I</u>
<u>don't have to save time for time</u>

<u>I like to see a beautiful black brother and sister</u>
<u>with no mixture pure and true. To me nothing can</u>
<u>compare because it's very rare.</u>

Never assume I mean something else, because I'm
not like that. Let me explain, although, I shouldn't
have too. I love the bone structure and pureness of

67

an African race, I guess I would feel the same way of any other culture of people. As they say, we are all a melting pot, however, I am an artist, and I admire beauty in my own beholder in me.

<u>Don't let my right be wrong, without first telling me how I wronged you.</u>

I like flirtatious comments that come from admiration, not salacious innuendo without rhyme or reason to motivate me.

I don't like to gossip, or gossiping woman, especially the ones that claim to be so godly and look down on others, yall might not like me after reading this, but oh well

I'm not perfect, and I do fall short, but I do try. I need to stay humble, and check my self. There is always room for improvement on my part.

When my creativity goes a part of me goes. Creativity will keep you going as long as you water it.

You can take the girl out the country, but you can't take the country out the girl. It's where my heart is.

An emotion is the expression of self. I have many emotions to protect each self. It will

take a lifetime to uncover the myths of me.
When you think you know me you don't.
Try and figure me out you won't.

Don't take my picture unless it's a good one.
I don't like nasty food or bad pictures,
Contrary to popular opinion, mirrors and
pictures don't always speak truth. You make
the picture, the picture does not make you.
Mirrors are just a way to fool you. Don't fall

for it be your own reflection of yourself not
what you think others think of you.

I just love to feel sexy most of the time. Then
again I like to feel casual. I just love being
me. Muah, kisses for me.

European nails like Jezebel , make up
highlighted her eyes to make them stand out.
May sound superficial, however, she thought
she was a butterfly before she died.

A woman that is innocent and sweet or sweet
without innocence , makes no difference if
that's what she chooses to be.

I am New York happy where Broadway Shows
and neon lights are until I get to Paris the
land of love.

Don't get me wrong, I'm still a country girl
who loves the farm, and wide open space , this
is where I'll be in the end jogging, drawing
writing and dancing.

Give me exotic soup, feed me with ingredients
from a far away land in Saigon. Bring me a
taste of mystery.   Let me make your life
more intriguing.

Cats are intriguing to me. Her name is Sasha
we complement each other, lioness and kitten.

<u>I close my eyes to ambivalence.   I meditate
and I am free, in the today and now, not the
yesterday that was me.</u>

<u>Take away my lit candle within that ignites
my smile, the way I walk and talk, but don't
take away my intuition that is my power by
definition to my resolve</u>

I would like a good husband to make me want
to be a very good wife.

I have to epitomize self and embody me to get
the full effect of an experience. It's not you,
it's just me or selfishness. When my mind
calls me to work I have to answer. Physically,
I feel regret, however, I wouldn't change it or

have it any other way. You just have to understand that I'm not changing. I am who I am. I am who I want to be. This is me.

I said I didn't do the crime. Clyde was dead before I got there. My name isn't Bonnie it's PJ smiling, blame it on my mind at that time not me, my wicked side. Ok I confess I used mommas gun. I said be gone was my only crime.

When I like what I am doing, I can do it all night. Yep I do it, do it, do it until I am satisfied. Hopefully, your mind wasn't in the gutter because I wasn't talking about sex, I know you don't believe me. This is my personality just me being me. I said it, I did it, because sometimes you got to hit it and quit it. I'm too sexy for myself. Lol I'm not that innocent. Can't touch this, old fashioned too, ha

When a woman has to pretend not to be strong that shit just wrong.

Say what, you wanna classify me, hell no. Then you wanna classify my child. Trust me you will regret it. I am coming back to classify you too. My Classification stamp says , dumb fucking school did this to you!

They want to dictate to you. Don't let them. Fuck those dictators.

TO INSPIRE AND MOTIVATE

Become a genie in a bottle, go where ever your imagination takes you. Snap your fingers and your there. Be sure to come back to reality.

I love it when I lose my thought and it comes back, it sure feels good when you know your mind is still all there.

For me to take back my words it's like I never really forgave, as if I'm holding a grudge. Sometimes you just want to take back your words, and say could you please just forget I said that.

They want to rob you of your mind and leave you with no food, feed them only what is needed and keep some for yourself.

I will not pretend that this world is so beautiful when the people in it have destroyed it. I will tell the truth the way I see it to be true.

I personify my today's thoughts and yesterdays memories, I am not the originator of yesterdays creation, nor the answer to tomorrows future only mine. All things possible thru Jah who sees all things and hears all things.

<u>Please let me sleep through the night with a clear conscious that's all I want.</u>

I am the cowboy who road that damn horse like a real woman. I even named my daughter Cheyanne and my son Shane. My hat reads Indian chief set my soul free. Indian blood reigns through me. A black Cherokee half breed Cowgirl that's me.

<u>I am New York, I have a New York hat. I like to go and get me some adventure and fill it once in a while.</u>

<u>*I'm smooth like butta & Crazy like a Fox*</u>

I am so happy that caffeine is my only bad habit, I admit it wasn't always that way, and my bad habits were , thank God, not that bad, I am harder on myself than I should be.

<u>I am the keeper of my own conquest.</u>
<u>What you seek you shall find.</u>

I am a black and red rose inside a deep red heart. Purple kisses is what I give. My heart bleeds tears with strong vines like a tree that are still growing and trying my best not to get choked.

<u>A rose inside a deep red heart bleeds a purple</u>
<u>kiss</u>

I like super bad ass high heels, they excite me but I don't wear red lipstick.

<u>I love the rich culture of Philadelphia, to me it's not rich but they do it like they are for the people.</u>

Sometimes I get tired. Then I realize I just needed some sleep. Sometimes I forget to eat then I realize I'm hungry. Most of the time I like to hear myself think spoken words.

If you can't beat them than make them love you. You don't have to join them. Be yourself without judging anyone. Queen B got sweet honey, that she catches them mean bullies with. It's true, I have to tell the truth.

I am in love with collard greens and beans.
Not giving them up either. I make stuffed
shells and macaroni and cheese to kill. My
children as well as my man stay happy .
I feed them with love.

Momma, that's me, likes dolls, they warm my
heart.. Little children in general make me
happy, especially babies. Could it be dolls were
my friends who helped protect me when I was
young. Hey I still have some little girl in me.

I believe I am a genius because small stuff
sometimes confuses me. My mind tends to
prioritize what it doesn't need, at least that is
my take on it. Believe it or not, I do. Ha Ha

TO INSPIRE AND MOTIVATE

I believe there is a big difference between being selfless and self perseverance, and a small difference between selfish and selfless. Usually no good deed is a selfless act.

I am the TLC group, Shaka Khan, Erica Badu, Jill Scott, Corinne Bailey Rae, Whitney Houston, yes, I said Whitney. Mary J. Blige, Keisha Cole and Leena James go in a different slot they are my girls. Patty Labelle for real for real. Sade, my girl I love you. However I'm really just PJ

My brother you need to show me something, so I know you are real. I need to feel what you are bringing to the table. What you got, come on give it to me. I like food that's hot not cold. Take the risk, give it your best.

I am riding darkness on a dark horse so you better watch out my shadow follows me . I am different and dangerous in a good way. Yes it's scary , yes I have a sword that's sharp , along with momma's gun. I suggest not to try me. My other side is most worthy of getting to know.

I have an intense desire to travel. I think I need a lot of money to do that, but I still enjoy the rich culture of Philly, excitement of New York and waves in AC. I really like riding the train on a clear day. Love the train.

Quote block can mean when you run out of things to say, you start telling your personal business be careful.

My Light of day shines through life's darkness.

When my creativity goes, a part of me goes.

<u>If you don't like me for who I am, than you don't have to like me at all.</u>

<u>I am entitled to spew a bunch of crap because I'm human.</u>

No shame in my game. Chicken feet, pig feet too, yep. My man don't eat pork so I will have to give it up, I think, I can do that??

I could be any athlete, I'd become a runner. Everything about a runner to me says determination, for now I'll settle for jogging, hey that's still running. The runner in me will never leave.

85

My hero is Harriet Tubman not because I am black, It's because she carries mommas gun, the same one I carry a rifle to get the job done, Don't try me or test my courage. I am a mother of children and a motivator. Moses delivered his people out from slavery . Let my people go wasn't only said with courage there was an underlying force behind the message . I am in inspired and motivated by her.

When it's so hot I'm just glad it won't get but so hot. The power of the sun, the wind and the rain is amazing.   Yes indeed.

I dance because I am happy and naturally sensual. A dancer knows how to let go.

QUOTES By Paula R. Jumper

Zoe Saldana played Avatar and wants to play Nina Simone, I feel guilty because I believe she is gorgeous and I don't care what nationality she is. I'm retracting if the personality is crap.

I feel like time stands still when get to watch old movies, I do know this shows my age, I'm alright with it though because I'm alright with me

Lord I am so glad I am a grown ass woman, I feel complete, If it wasn't for my age I wouldn't be even with my flaws.

Skateboards and drawing that is all I wanted as a child. Things in the world have really changed a lot.

"Who do I trust, I trust me". I am a bad ass like the movie Scar Face , we both like quotes, ha

Please let me sleep through the night with a clear conscious that's all I want.

Don't let your daughters listen to the song , Giving Him Something He Can Feel from the movie Sparkle , they might get pregnant like I did, naww just kidding, maybe not, ha ha

She is like a kitten, but looks in the mirror and sees a lion. I stole this from somewhere I couldn't help it because it is so me I had to have it.

I hope today is as good as yesterday, and tomorrow as good as today.

Nothing detests me more than not knowing what is detestable is disgusting. What is easily digested may be hard to expel.

When I'm moving too fast, life has a way of slowing me down, it's called being really tired but grateful.

I love a sweet morning. What is sweeter than an early morning, not even darkness or a little rain?

If you believe your true identity was a hidden revelation, than you're probably really nerdy like me, only I am a kick ass nerd, ha ha it's true

I f I allow you to get to know me consider it a privilege, there is only one me.

I like to separate my mind from my body and let my intuition carry me like an Eagle in the sky. Look for me I will be somewhere flying or perched by a tree next to the sea just chilling and waiting to make my move.

My imagination constantly changes, you will never really know me like I know myself.

Don't let my shyness fool you, I am no fool for you to take to school.

I am not justified by a man, I justify me by my own actions, whether right or wrong, and I don't have to sacrifice my strength to prove my femininity to no one and that is a fact.

When people can't see my worth, I always know that I am worth way more than they can see.

I am learning that I cannot hide from my age.
It's gonna catch me. I think it's gonna have to
slow down for another five years before I give
in.

Sometimes I have to step outside of myself to
see who really needs me is me.

I am a multifaceted person, I like to reach
different facets of a person so I can learn
something.

If I said Soul Jah of God you would like me, If
I said sister Souljah, you probably won't,
Politics and religion, you can't have both or
can you?

I gave up curse words for the word revolution, and now I'm supposed to change it to turning point and tipping point. I don't think so! I'm no politician, but I'll fight for women and children in a second. A man too if he supports us. I'm no feminist, but I'd like to be an advocate that inspires.

Yes I am photogenic I know this, but the truth is I speak artistic expression. Look at me and tell me what I am saying.

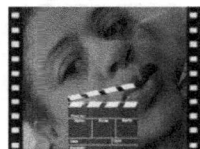

My kiss is not an ordinary kiss. read my lips
they are purple and always kissable.

A rose inside a deep red heart bleeds a purple kiss.

<u>I have two sides one side likes to fight. One side is a good person. I chose to let God handle the bad people because I know that they can't beat him.</u>

My beginning to my end is no longer my end to my beginning.

QUOTES By Paula R. Jumper

This is me standing on the steps of the Franklin Institute in Philadelphia at the Dead Sea Scrolls exhibition in Philadelphia. I was determined to be there. I want to say that being in the presence of the original scrolls was the best feeling ever. The magnitude of the experience is beyond explanation. It really was a once in a life endeavor, and to have it come right to our back yard. I still haven't realized how great of an experience it is because it's hard for me to find the words too or appreciate such a blessing. My youngest son is taking the picture. I would have liked to have taken more of my family. If the chance ever comes again I promise I will cease the opportunity, and let everyone know as well.

My eyes can see right through you, although you will never know it that they are the window to my thinking.

QUOTES By Paula R. Jumper

Two species that come together and made
better is good. It's not one dimensional
anymore

99

PLEASE SMILE FOR ME TODAY

ACKNOWLEDGEMENT

If you would like to write a review or acknowledgement, please feel free to send to my personal email address at paulypj22@yahoo.com A website will soon be available to place your comments. Thank you, to all my fans, and people who I may have inspired.

PUBLISHED

COMING SOON

Being Beautiful Dark Shadowess Part 2
Poetry and Writings
By
Paula R. Jumper

FLOWER CHILD
A Memoir of
A Flower Child by
Paula R. Jumper

Quotes to inspire and Motivate focuses on motivational thoughts, life's experiences, and Inspirational moments. Paula would like to encourage people to give encouragement to others while really meaning what they say. She feels it does make a difference, and can indeed boost confidence when needed.

Paula is a proud mother of three children and one grandson. She is also a proud owner of her of her dog Bart and cat. Sasha. To add to her interest, and endeavors, Paula is an aspiring Portrait and design Artist.

Paula hopes to be an inspiration to others through her aspirations, as well as motivate people to love themselves and spread the love. Appreciating the platform given is her way of connecting with people, by sharing her writings and stories, including her poetry that are very dear to her heart.